SPAIN

By Theia Lake and Joanne Mattern

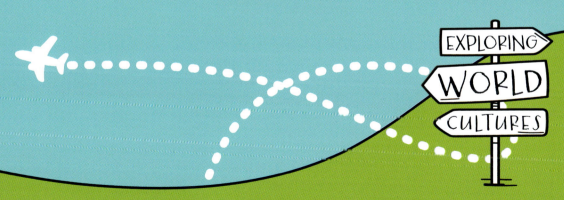

Published in 2025 by Cavendish Square Publishing, LLC
2544 Clinton Street, Buffalo, NY 14224

Copyright © 2025 by Cavendish Square Publishing, LLC

Second Edition

No part of this publication may be reproduced, stored in a retrieval system, or transmitted in any form or by any means—electronic, mechanical, photocopying, recording, or otherwise—without the prior permission of the copyright owner. Request for permission should be addressed to Permissions, Cavendish Square Publishing, 2544 Clinton Street, Buffalo, NY 14224. Tel (877) 980-4450; fax (877) 980-4454.

Website: cavendishsq.com

This publication represents the opinions and views of the author based on their personal experience, knowledge, and research. The information in this book serves as a general guide only. The author and publisher have used their best efforts in preparing this book and disclaim liability rising directly or indirectly from the use and application of this book.

All websites were available and accurate when this book was sent to press.

Library of Congress Cataloging-in-Publication Data

Names: Lake, Theia, author. | Mattern, Joanne, 1963- Spain.
Title: Spain / Theia Lake.
Description: Second edition. | Buffalo, NY : Cavendish Square Publishing,
  [2025] | Series: Exploring world cultures | Includes index.
Identifiers: LCCN 2024009644 (print) | LCCN 2024009645 (ebook) | ISBN
  9781502670861 (library binding) | ISBN 9781502670854 (paperback) | ISBN
  9781502670878 (ebook)
Subjects: LCSH: Spain--Juvenile literature.
Classification: LCC DP17 .L35 2025 (print) | LCC DP17 (ebook) | DDC
  946--dc23/eng/20240315
LC record available at https://lccn.loc.gov/2024009644
LC ebook record available at https://lccn.loc.gov/2024009645

Writers: Joanne Mattern; Theia Lake (second edition)
Editor: Theresa Emminizer
Copyeditor: Danielle Haynes
Designer: Andrea Davison-Bartolotta

The photographs in this book are used by permission and through the courtesy of: Cover Tomsickova Tatyana/Shutterstock.com; p. 4 Eszter Szadeczky-Kardoss/Shutterstock.com; p. 5 Marcos del Mazo/Shutterstock.com; p. 6 frees/Shutterstock.com; p. 7 Pawel Kazmierczak/Shutterstock.com; p. 8 aquatarkus/Shutterstock.com; p. 9 EQRoy/Shutterstock.com; p. 10 OSCAR GONZALEZ FUENTES/Shutterstock.com; p. 11 Natursports/Shutterstock.com; p. 12 LiliGraphie/Shutterstock.com; p. 13 joserpizarro/Shutterstock.com; p. 15 (top) Helecho_Mad/Shutterstock.com; p. 15 (bottom) Robert Bertold/Shutterstock.com; p. 16 Laiotz/Shutterstock.com; p. 17 leonardo2011/Shutterstock.com; pp. 18, 23 nito/Shutterstock.com; p. 19 jorisvo/Shutterstock.com; p. 20 Aleksandar Todorovic/Shutterstock.com; p. 21 Armando Oliveira/Shutterstock.com; p. 22 JoeLogan/Shutterstock.com; p. 24 Georgios Tsichlis/Shutterstock.com; p. 25 Helena GARCIA HUERTAS/Shutterstock.com; p. 26 bodrumsurf/Shutterstock.com; p. 27 David Pineda Svenske/Shutterstock.com; p. 28 Pat_Hastings/Shutterstock.com; p. 29 mythja/Shutterstock.com.

Some of the images in this book illustrate individuals who are models. The depictions do not imply actual situations or events.

CPSIA compliance information: Batch #CS25CSQ: For further information contact Cavendish Square Publishing LLC at 1-877-980-4450.

Printed in the United States of America

CONTENTS

Introduction 4
Chapter 1   Geography 6
Chapter 2   History 8
Chapter 3   Government 10
Chapter 4   The Economy 12
Chapter 5   The Environment 14
Chapter 6   The People Today 16
Chapter 7   Lifestyle 18
Chapter 8   Religion 20
Chapter 9   Language 22
Chapter 10 Arts and Festivals 24
Chapter 11 Fun and Play 26
Chapter 12 Food 28
Glossary 30
Find Out More 31
Index 32

INTRODUCTION

Spain is a beautiful country in southwestern Europe. It has a long history, dating back many thousands of years. Spain became a leading world power during the 1500s, when it built a large **empire** through many overseas **conquests**. The legacy, or lasting effect, of these conquests can still be felt. Today, the Spanish language is the second-most spoken language in the world.

Madrid is the capital of Spain.

Spain is a land of many rich **traditions**. The lively music, graceful dancing, and colorful artwork are just some of the many things that make this country so special. Every year, thousands of people travel to Spain to enjoy the tasty food and sandy beaches. They also come to see the historic cities, such as Madrid and Barcelona, and take part in the fun festivals, or celebrations.

Spain is truly a place like no other. Read on to find out more about this interesting country!

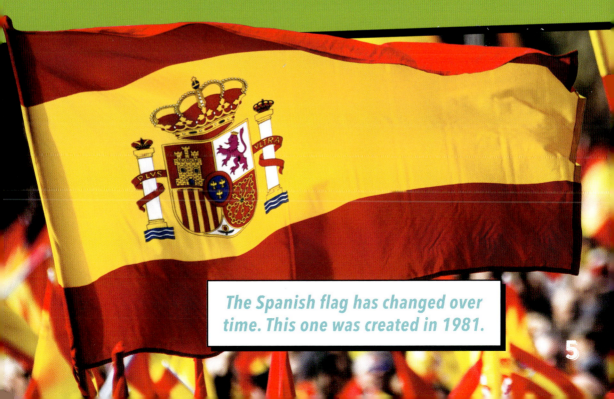

The Spanish flag has changed over time. This one was created in 1981.

GEOGRAPHY

Spain is located on an area of land called the Iberian Peninsula. A peninsula is a piece of land that's almost completely surrounded by water. Spain is surrounded by the Mediterranean Sea, the Atlantic Ocean, and the Bay of Biscay. Spain is separated from Africa by a narrow body of water called the Strait of Gibraltar.

Spain shares the Iberian Peninsula with the country of Portugal.

Spain has many sunny beaches.

FACT! Spain is the fourth-largest country in Europe. It covers 195,124 square miles (505,370 square kilometers).

Spain is also bordered by three countries: Portugal, France, and Andorra. The Canary Islands and the Balearic Islands are also part of Spain.

MANY MOUNTAINS

Most of Spain is made up of a high plateau, or flat land, called the Meseta. There are also lowlands along the coast. However, Spain also has several mountain ranges. The most important mountain ranges are the Pyrenees and the Cantabrian ranges. Thick forests grow along the sides of these mountains.

HISTORY

People have been living in Spain since prehistoric times—before written history. During the 1400s and 1500s, Spain was a leading world power. Its kings and queens sent **explorers** to other parts of the world and claimed land there.

PREHISTORY

Bones from some of the earliest known humans in Western Europe have been found in Spain. They belong to Neanderthals, a species, or kind, of humans that died out completely. People may have been living in Spain as many as 1.2 million years ago.

Isabella I ruled Spain with her husband Ferdinand II from 1474 until her death in 1504. Her sculpture stands near the Royal Palace of Madrid.

During the 1600s, Spain lost some of its power. It fought in several wars. Between 1936 and 1939, the Spanish Civil War tore Spain apart. After the war, a **dictator** named Francisco Franco ruled Spain. Franco died in 1975. The country made a new **constitution** in 1978.

FACT! At the height of its power, the Kingdom of Spain ruled places on five different continents, or landmasses.

Prehistoric cave and rock art has been found in Spain. Replicas, or remakes, of this art can be seen at the National Museum and Research Center of Altamira.

GOVERNMENT

Spain's new constitution stated that Spain is a constitutional monarchy. That means that Spain's monarch (king or queen) is the head of the state. However, the monarch doesn't have real power.

The prime minister is the head of the government. They have a cabinet, or group of officials who help them.

Felipe VI is the monarch of Spain today.

Spain is broken up into 17 autonomous, or self-governing, communities. Each community has its own capital city. Spain also has two autonomous cities in Africa: Ceuta and Melilla.

FACT! Spain's monarchy is hereditary. That means it's passed down from one member of a family to another.

All Spanish citizens over 18 years old have the right to vote.

PARLIAMENT

The Spanish government also includes two groups, or houses, of Parliament. Members of Parliament are elected by the people. They make laws. The Supreme Court is a group of judges. It makes sure all the laws are fair.

THE ECONOMY

A country's economy is the way in which goods and services are made, sold, and used there. Historically, Spain has had a very strong economy.

Spain's economy is based on agriculture, or farming, as well as mining and service work. Spain's main crops are cereals, olives, oranges, grapes, and cotton. Some farmers raise cattle, sheep, and pigs. Spanish mines produce iron, coal, and copper.

Spanish currency, or money, is called the euro. Euros are used in several European countries.

Most people in Spain work in service jobs. They work at banks, restaurants, stores, hotels, and more. Tourism, which is the business of travel, is a big part of Spain's economy too.

TOURISM

Millions of tourists travel to Spain to see its beaches and islands. Others visit the country's beautiful mountains or enjoy its city life. Tourism brings in billions of dollars every year.

FACT!
Spain has the 14th-largest economy in the world. It's considered a high-*income* economy.

The Bank of Spain is in Seville.

THE ENVIRONMENT

Spain's mountains, rivers, and coasts are home to many beautiful plants and animals. Rabbits, birds, and foxes live in the grasslands. Eagles, vultures, and a type of goat called a chamois live on the rocky cliffs and mountains. Colorful songbirds are found in Spanish gardens and woods.

Spain's rivers and wetlands are full of water birds, mammals, fish, and reptiles. Fish and other sea creatures fill the Mediterranean Sea and the Atlantic Ocean.

Many plants and animals are protected, or kept safe, in Spain's national parks.

NATIONAL PARKS

There are 16 national parks in Spain. The country began making national parks in 1918, long before many other European countries did. Teide National Park is the most-visited national park in Spain, drawing around 4 million visitors each year.

Spain is home to the Iberian lynx. It's an endangered species (at risk of dying out), with fewer than 300 animals in the wild.

FACT!
The red carnation is the national flower of Spain. It commonly grows in southern parts of the country.

Mount Teide is a volcano in the Canary Islands. It's the highest point in Spain.

THE PEOPLE TODAY

People who live in Spain are called Spanish or Spaniards. They come from many different **ethnic** backgrounds.

Some of the ethnic groups in Spain include Basque, Castilian, Catalan, and Galician. These groups are native to different parts of the country. They traditionally have different languages, music, artwork, clothing, and celebrations.

FACT!
There are about 47 million people living in Spain today.

These dancers are doing a traditional Basque folk dance.

Roma are another ethnic group in Spain. They travel from place to place. Most of Spain's cities have large Roma populations.

Because Spain is close to northern Africa, people have moved to Spain from Morocco, which is in Africa.

FAMILY LIFE

Most Spanish families are made up of parents and one or two children. Children often live with their parents until they get married in their 20s or 30s. Families usually eat meals together. In cities, families often live in apartments.

In this picture, Spaniards are enjoying a day out eating at restaurants in the city of León.

LIFESTYLE

Family, food, and relaxation are important parts of life in Spain. Spaniards believe in the importance of enjoying life. They may go to work or school until the middle of the afternoon. Then, many businesses close for a midday time of rest. The attention given to having a healthy balance between work and life beyond work is part of what sets Spain apart from other countries.

FACT! Traditional Spanish clothing is usually brightly colored, with beautiful **designs**. Women may wear long dresses, and men wear short jackets and wide hats.

These friends are relaxing together in a park in Barcelona.

Traditional flamenco dresses hang outside a house in Andalusia.

Most Spaniards today wear western-style clothing that you might see in America, such as jeans and dresses. However, some traditional clothing can still be seen.

SIESTA

A siesta is a Spanish tradition of taking an afternoon nap following lunch. The siesta goes back to earlier times, when people who worked on farms would rest during the hottest hours of the day. Today, most Spaniards don't take siestas.

RELIGION

The **Roman Catholic** religion, or belief system, has been a big part of Spanish history. In the past, everyone had to follow that religion. However, in 1978, when the new constitution was made, it gave Spanish people the freedom to follow any religion. Today, most people in Spain are still members of the Roman Catholic religion.

There are many beautiful churches in Spain. This is the Cathedral of Saint Mary in Seville.

Because so many people in Spain are Catholic, religious holidays are celebrated throughout the country. Christmas, Easter, and Three Kings Day are some of the most important holidays. Many children also go to Catholic schools.

THE CAMINO DE SANTIAGO

A pilgrimage is a journey to a religious site. The Camino de Santiago is a famous pilgrim trail in Spain, dating back to **medieval** times. It ends at the Cathedral of Santiago de Compostela, where Saint James was buried.

FACT! Spain also has small populations that follow other religions. These religions include Judaism and Islam. Islam is now the fastest-growing religion in Spain.

This person is walking the Camino de Santiago (Way of Saint James) trail.

LANGUAGE

Spanish is the official language of Spain. It's also called Castilian. Castilian Spanish is taught in schools and used at home and at work. It is also spoken by people on television and the radio.

FACT! Around 450 million people around the world speak Spanish. It's the official language of 20 different countries.

Spanish children may also learn English or French in school.

Not everyone speaks Castilian Spanish. People who live in Catalonia speak Catalan. Catalan Spanish is different from Castilian Spanish. So is Galician Spanish, which is spoken in part of western Spain. There are many other languages as well, including Aragonese, Asturian, and Leonese.

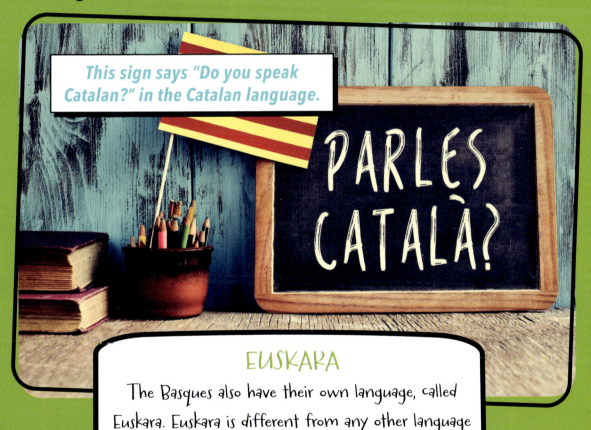

This sign says "Do you speak Catalan?" in the Catalan language.

EUSKARA

The Basques also have their own language, called Euskara. Euskara is different from any other language spoken in Europe. There are around 750,000 Euskara speakers in the world. It's most widely spoken in Gipuzkoa, a place in the Basque Country of Spain.

ARTS AND FESTIVALS

Spain is the birthplace of many wonderful artists, such as Pablo Picasso and Salvador Dali. Miguel de Cervantes, writer of *Don Quixote*, is probably the most well-known Spanish author.

Dance is also very popular in Spain. Traditional Spanish music is very lively. It includes guitars, drums, castanets, and other instruments. Traditional Spanish dances include the flamenco, the fandango, and the paso doble.

FACT!
Thousands of visitors travel to Spain to see and take part in the wonderful festivals there.

Antoni Gaudi was a Spanish architect, or building designer. His work can be seen in Barcelona.

There are many festivals, or celebrations, in Spain. Carnival and La Tomatina are some of the biggest. Carnival includes colorful clothing, parades, and parties. La Tomatina includes a big, messy tomato fight!

THE RUNNING OF THE BULLS

One of the most famous events in Spain is the Running of the Bulls. This is held during the Festival of San Fermín. Every July, bulls run through the streets of Pamplona. Thousands of people come to see the bulls and even run with them.

Artists make amazing paper figures for the Las Fallas festival held in Valencia each year.

FUN AND PLAY

People in Spain spend a lot of time enjoying the sun. People take walks and go hiking. Those who live near the coast often enjoy a day at the beach. Swimming and fishing are popular ways to have fun.

FACT!
Bullfighting has a long history in Spain, but many people believe it to be cruel, or unkind, to the bulls.

Fans go to Camp Nou Stadium in Barcelona to watch FC (Fútbol Club) Barcelona matches.

Sports are a big part of Spanish life. Soccer, or *fútbol*, is the most popular sport. Each city has its own team, and thousands of fans go to games. Kids play fútbol with their friends too.

OTHER SPORTS

Motor sports, basketball, tennis, golf, and handball are other top sports in Spain. Many Formula One racing drivers, including Fernando Alonso, have come from Spain. Spaniard Rafael Nadal is one of the greatest tennis players of all time.

Bullfighting is a traditional Spanish sport.

FOOD

Paella is probably the most famous Spanish food. Paella is a tasty dish filled with rice, meat, vegetables, and spices. Paella may include different foods depending on where it's made. Some areas use fish or shrimp. Other places use beef, chicken, or pork.

FACT! Tapas are small plates of food that are often served with drinks in Spanish bars.

Gazpacho is a cold tomato soup eaten in Spain.

In the Basque area, *pintxo* is a small dish eaten as a snack with wine. Pintxos have a skewer, or stick, in them.

Spanish ham is some of the best in the world. Croquetas de Jamón are a fried dish made with ham.

SWEET TREATS

Spanish people often like sweet desserts. Churros are long sticks of fried dough that are covered in sugar and dipped in chocolate. Flan is a creamy dessert. Tarta de Santiago is a tasty almond cake.

Spain is the world's largest producer of olives! Many Spanish dishes include olives.

GLOSSARY

constitution: The basic laws by which a country, state, or group is governed.

conquest: The act of conquering, or taking control over, a place.

design: A decorative pattern. Also, a drawing of something that is being planned or created.

dictator: A person who rules a country with total power and often in a harmful way.

empire: A group of lands and peoples under one ruler.

ethnic: Of or relating to large groups of people who have the same cultural background and ways of life.

explorer: Someone who travels to a new place to find out more about it.

income: The payment or money received for doing a job.

medieval: Relating to the Middle Ages (5th century to 15th century CE).

Roman Catholic: A branch of Christianity led by the pope.

tradition: A way of thinking, behaving, or doing something that's been used by people in a particular society for a long time.

FIND OUT MORE

Books

Noble, Isabella, Stuart Butler, Natalia Diaz, Jamie Ditaranto, and Esme Fox. *Lonely Planet Spain*. Oakland, CA: Lonely Planet Publishing, 2023.

Van, R.L. *Spain*. Minneapolis, MN: Big Buddy Books, 2023

Websites

National Geographic Kids: Spain
kids.nationalgeographic.com/geography/countries/article/spain
Learn more about the history, people, and environment of Spain.

Spanish Tourism
www.spain.info/en/
Discover all there is to see and do in Spain.

Video

Spain: Tomatina Festival
www.youtube.com/watch?v=8oQSwBb5jUQ&t=8s
Watch a video about the Tomatina Festival in Buñol.

Publisher's note to educators and parents: Our editors have carefully reviewed these websites to ensure that they are suitable for students. Many websites change frequently, however, and we cannot guarantee that a site's future contents will continue to meet our high standards of quality and educational value. Be advised that students should be closely supervised whenever they access the internet.

INDEX

A
agriculture, 12
arts, 5, 9, 16, 24, 25

B
Balearic Islands, 7

C
Canary Islands, 7, 15
clothing, 18, 19
cuisine, 17, 18, 28, 29

E
economy, 12, 13
education, 18, 21, 22
empire, 4, 8, 9
ethnicity, 16, 17

F
Felipe VI (king), 10
Ferdinand II (king), 8
Franco, Francisco, 9

G
government, 9, 10, 11, 20

I
Iberian Peninsula, 6
Isabella I (queen), 8

L
language, 4, 16, 22, 23

M
marriage, 17
Mediterranean Sea, 6, 14
Mount Teide, 15

P
plants, 7, 14, 15

R
religion, 20, 21

S
Spanish Civil War, 9
sports, 26, 27
Strait of Gibraltar, 6

T
Teide National Park, 14
tourism, 5, 13, 24

W
wildlife, 14, 15